COMPASSIONATE RESPECT